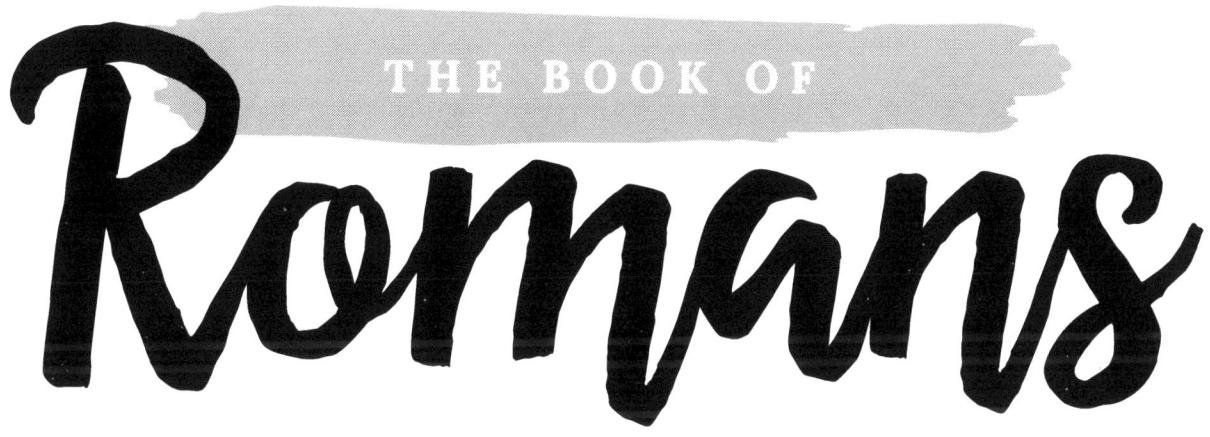

THE BOOK OF Romans

ONE CHAPTER A DAY

GoodMorningGirls.org

The Book of Romans

© 2016 Women Living Well Ministries, LLC

ALL RIGHTS RESERVED

No part of this book may be reproduced in any form or by any electronic or mechanical means, including information storage and retrieval systems, without written permission from the author, except in the case of a reviewer, who may quote brief passages embodied in critical articles or in a review.

Scripture is from the ESV® Bible (The Holy Bible, English Standard Version®), copyright © 2001 by Crossway Bibles, a publishing ministry of Good News Publishers. Used by permission. All rights reserved.

Welcome to Good Morning Girls! We are so glad you are joining us.

God created us to walk with Him, to know Him, and to be loved by Him. He is our living well, and when we drink from the water He continually provides, His living water will change the entire course of our lives.

Jesus said: "Whoever drinks of the water that I will give him will never be thirsty again. The water that I will give him will become in him a spring of water welling up to eternal life." ~ John 4:14 (ESV)

So let's begin.

The method we use here at GMG is called the **SOAK** method.

- ❒ **S**—The S stands for *Scripture*—Read the chapter for the day. Then choose 1-2 verses and write them out word for word. (There is no right or wrong choice—just let the Holy Spirit guide you.)

- ❒ **O**—The O stands for *Observation*—Look at the verse or verses you wrote out. Write 1 or 2 observations. What stands out to you? What do you learn about the character of God from these verses? Is there a promise, command or teaching?

- ❒ **A**—The A stands for *Application*—Personalize the verses. What is God saying to you? How can you apply them to your life? Are there any changes you need to make or an action to take?

- ❒ **K**—The K stands for *Kneeling in Prayer*—Pause, kneel and pray. Confess any sin God has revealed to you today. Praise God for His word. Pray the passage over your own life or someone you love. Ask God to help you live out your applications.

SOAK God's word into your heart and squeeze every bit of nourishment you can out of each day's scripture reading. Soon you will find your life transformed by the renewing of your mind!

Walk with the King!

Courtney

WomenLivingWell.org, GoodMorningGirls.org

Join the GMG Community

Share your daily SOAK at 7:45am on **Facebook.com/GoodMorningGirlsWLW**

Instagram: WomenLivingWell #GoodMorningGirls

GMG Bible Coloring Chart

COLORS	KEYWORDS
PURPLE	God, Jesus, Holy Spirit, Saviour, Messiah
PINK	women of the Bible, family, marriage, parenting, friendship, relationships
RED	love, kindness, mercy, compassion, peace, grace
GREEN	faith, obedience, growth, fruit, salvation, fellowship, repentance
YELLOW	worship, prayer, praise, doctrine, angels, miracles, power of God, blessings
BLUE	wisdom, teaching, instruction, commands
ORANGE	prophecy, history, times, places, kings, genealogies, people, numbers, covenants, vows, visions, oaths, future
BROWN/GRAY	Satan, sin, death, hell, evil, idols, false teachers, hypocrisy, temptation

Introduction to the Book of Romans

In the book of Romans, the apostle Paul, comes to the gospel's defense. Before his salvation, Paul was a Pharisee of Pharisees - he knew the law, and he knew it well. Yet, after an encounter with Christ, he was forever changed. He went from persecuting the church to proclaiming the gospel. Like a skilled lawyer, he sent his defense of the gospel to the believers in Rome.

Paul had never met these believers but he felt kindred to them as brothers and sisters in Christ.

After an introduction, Paul presents the facts of the gospel and declares allegiance to it. His case is firm. Salvation is available to all, regardless of their identity, sin or heritage. He proclaims that we are saved by grace through faith. He explains the concept of grace and faith - that grace is unmerited favor and that faith is complete trust in the finished work of Christ on the cross.

Other words like justification (or justify) and sanctification are used and defined. He explains that we can be free from the power of sin and free from the dominion of the law. We are free to live in Christ and like Christ - this is true freedom!

Then, Paul addresses the Jewish believer specifically that is in Rome. He explains that God has made a way for both the Jew and the Gentile.

Paul ends the book talking about living in submission to Christ, and how we can use our gifts to serve others and point them back to salvation. Paul stresses the idea of unity- especially between the Jew and the Gentile.

As we read the book of Romans, we can reexamine the commitment we have made to Christ. If you have never committed your life to Him - this book will give you a clear understanding of why you should and how to surrender your life to Him.

Key Verse: *"I am not ashamed of the gospel, for it is the power of God for salvation to everyone who believes."* Romans 1:16

Date Written: about AD 57

Writer: Paul

Themes:

Sin: Sin means refusing to do God's will and failing to do all that God wants.

We have all sinned and fallen short of the glory of God. We all need salvation from our sin. Sin came into the world when Adam rebelled against God. Our nature is to rebel against God as well. Because of our sin, we are separated from God. No matter how good we try to be, or how hard we try to "live right" - we cannot earn salvation. Only Christ can save us.

Salvation: Our sin points us to a need for a Savior.

Sin points to our need for being cleansed and forgiven. God, in his kindness and great love, made a way of salvation through Christ's death that paid the penalty for our sins. This is the gospel- the good news! We must believe in Christ and that he forgave us of our sins, in order to enter a relationship with God.

Growth: What happens after salvation? Does God leave us where we were? No! We grow in our relationship with God.

We are set apart for God and His service. Because we are free from sin, we are also now free to grow to become more like Christ.

Service: After salvation, we are to serve God.

We are to give God credit and glory for what He has done in our lives. Serving God unifies all believers.

I'm so excited to begin the book of Romans with you. This book will take us back to the basics and the fundamentals of our faith. While the gospel is simple enough for a 5 year old to understand, its depths can be explored for a lifetime and never grow old. As we go chapter by chapter and verse by verse systematically through the book of Romans, the key truths of sin, salvation and how deeply we are loved by Jesus will leap off of the pages and into our hearts and change us making us more like Christ.

Let's get started.

Keep walking with the King!

Special Thanks

I want to extend a special thank you to Mandy Kelly, Rosilind Jukic, Bridget Childress and Misty Leask for your help with this journal. Your love, dedication and leadership to the Good Morning Girls ministry is such a blessing to all. Thank you for giving to the Lord.

~ Courtney

I am not ashamed of the gospel,

for it is the power of God for salvation

to everyone who believes.

Romans 1:16

Reflection Question:

Describe a time when you were ashamed to admit or share your faith with someone.

How do you wish you had handled that situation differently?

Romans 1

S—The S stands for *Scripture*

O—The O stands for *Observation*

A—The A stands for *Application*

K—The K stands for *Kneeling in Prayer*

God's kindness

is meant to lead you to repentance.

Romans 2:4

Reflection Question:

The kindness of God is meant to lead us to repentance.

How has God's kindness led you to repentance? And who can you be kind to today, in hopes of leading them to repentance?

Romans 2

S—The S stands for *Scripture*

O—The O stands for *Observation*

A—The A stands for *Application*

K—The K stands for *Kneeling in Prayer*

For all have sinned and fall short of the glory of God.

Romans 3:23

Reflection Question:

There is no room for self-righteousness in the family of God. All of us are sinners and have fallen short of God's standard but through our faith in Jesus, we are redeemed!

Write your testimony. When did you realize for the first time that you were a sinner in need of Jesus and his saving grace?

Romans 3

S—The S stands for *Scripture*

O—The O stands for *Observation*

A—The A stands for *Application*

K—The K stands for *Kneeling in Prayer*

> *His faith was counted to him as righteousness.*
>
> *Romans 4:22*

Reflection Question:

Today we were reminded that Abraham remained faithful even though he had to wait to receive what was promised to him by God. His faith made him righteous.

What is it that you are waiting on and how strong is your faith today?

Romans 4

S—The S stands for **Scripture**

O—The O stands for **Observation**

A—The A stands for **Application**

K—The K stands for **Kneeling in Prayer**

*But God shows his love for us
in that while we were still sinners,
Christ died for us.*

Romans 5:8

Reflection Question:

Even in our weak sinful nature, Christ died for us!

Think back to the life that you had before Christ, how has it changed?

Romans 5

S—The S stands for **Scripture**

O—The O stands for **Observation**

A—The A stands for **Application**

K—The K stands for **Kneeling in Prayer**

What then?

Are we to sin because we

are not under law

but under grace?

By no means!

Romans 6:15

Reflection Question:

As Christians, we live under grace.

How does this give you the strength to rid yourself of things that God is convicting you to release, so you can serve Him better?

Romans 6

S—The S stands for **Scripture**

O—The O stands for **Observation**

A—The A stands for **Application**

K—The K stands for **Kneeling in Prayer**

For I know that nothing good dwells in me, that is, in my flesh. For I have the desire to do what is right, but not the ability to carry it out.

Romans 7:18

Reflection Question:

Though we are made new in Christ, all of us struggle with sin in our lives.

What is one thing you know is right to do but you struggle to live out in your life?

Romans 7

S—The S stands for **Scripture**

O—The O stands for **Observation**

A—The A stands for **Application**

K—The K stands for **Kneeling in Prayer**

And we know that for those who love God all things work together for good, for those who are called according to his purpose.

Romans 8:28

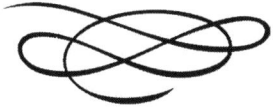

Reflection Question:

God is always at work in our lives bringing about his purpose and good.

How does knowing that His plans are good, for those who love him, bring you peace and comfort today?

Romans 8

S—The S stands for *Scripture*

O—The O stands for *Observation*

A—The A stands for *Application*

K—The K stands for *Kneeling in Prayer*

> *Those who were not my people*
> *I will call 'my people,'*
> *and her who was not beloved*
> *I will call 'beloved.'*
>
> *Romans 9:25*

Reflection Question:

It is the grace of God that allows us to be called 'his people' and 'his beloved.'

What have you learned about God's grace so far in our study of the book of Romans? Take a moment to write a prayer of thanks to God for His abundant grace.

Romans 9

S—The S stands for *Scripture*

O—The O stands for *Observation*

A—The A stands for *Application*

K—The K stands for *Kneeling in Prayer*

If you confess with your mouth

that Jesus is Lord

and believe in your heart

that God raised him from the dead,

you will be saved.

Romans 10:9

Reflection Question:

Who was the first person that introduced you to Jesus?

Who was the first person that you introduced to Jesus?

Romans 10

S—The S stands for *Scripture*

O—The O stands for *Observation*

A—The A stands for *Application*

K—The K stands for *Kneeling in Prayer*

*Oh, the depth of the riches
and wisdom and knowledge of God!
How unsearchable are his judgments
and how inscrutable his ways!*

Romans 11:33

Reflection Question:

Sometimes it is hard to understand God's ways. God's ways are so much higher than man's.

How does knowing God's depth of riches, wisdom and knowledge comfort you, as you seek to follow Him and His Word?

Romans 11

S—The S stands for **Scripture**

O—The O stands for **Observation**

A—The A stands for **Application**

K—The K stands for **Kneeling in Prayer**

If possible, so far as it depends on you, live peaceably with all.

Romans 12:18

Reflection Question:

One of the marks of a believer is peace.

What are some ways that you can show Christian love and peace, to those who are being difficult in your life today?

Romans 12

S—The S stands for *Scripture*

O—The O stands for *Observation*

A—The A stands for *Application*

K—The K stands for *Kneeling in Prayer*

Owe no one anything,

except to love each other,

for the one who loves another

has fulfilled the law.

Romans 13:8

Reflection Question:

The second greatest commandment is that we love one another.

Who do you "owe" love to today? Write down a way that you can show love to this person this week.

Romans 13

S—The S stands for **Scripture**

O—The O stands for **Observation**

A—The A stands for **Application**

K—The K stands for **Kneeling in Prayer**

Let us not pass judgment

on one another any longer,

but rather decide never to put a stumbling block

or hindrance in the way of a brother.

Romans 14:13

Reflection Question:

A stumbling block is someone who is a more mature believer, who takes liberty in their choices, and then causes a younger believer to fall.

In what ways can you make sure that you are not becoming a stumbling block to another believer?

Romans 14

S—The S stands for *Scripture*

O—The O stands for *Observation*

A—The A stands for *Application*

K—The K stands for *Kneeling in Prayer*

May the God of hope

fill you with all joy and peace in believing,

so that by the power of the Holy Spirit

you may abound in hope.

Romans 15:13

Reflection Question:

Jesus is the hope of the Jews and the Gentiles.

Share how your hope in Jesus is lived out in your daily life.

Romans 15

S—The S stands for **Scripture**

O—The O stands for **Observation**

A—The A stands for **Application**

K—The K stands for **Kneeling in Prayer**

I appeal to you, brothers, to watch out for those who cause divisions and create obstacles contrary to the doctrine that you have been taught; avoid them.

Romans 16:17

Reflection Question:

We are to love people but we are also to love truth. While we are to avoid divisions, we are also called to avoid those who cause division. This is not an easy teaching.

How do you guard yourself against those who cause division between you and your beliefs?

Romans 16

S—The S stands for **Scripture**

O—The O stands for **Observation**

A—The A stands for **Application**

K—The K stands for **Kneeling in Prayer**

Made in the USA
Lexington, KY
15 January 2018